May, 2009

Joyce,

With best wishes for
your ongoing success.

Joe Calhoon

ON THE SAME PAGE

How to Engage Employees and Accelerate Growth

Joe Calhoon & Bruce Jeffrey

ISBN   978-1-60013-266-7

Publishing by
Insight Publishing
647 Wall Street • Sevierville, Tennessee • 37862

10 9 8 7 6 5 4 3 2

DEDICATION

WE EXTEND OUR DEEPEST APPRECIATION to our clients, families, mentors, vendors, and friends. Without the contributions of thousands of gracious souls, we would not be learning and teaching. It is our pleasure to partner in progress with you!

We are especially grateful to all of those whose stories are told in these pages. These caring and committed leaders are engaging their employees and building better businesses. Due to numerous personal, organizational, and marketplace factors, no one knows what might happen to these businesses in the future. What we do know is that these business leaders have created good jobs, helped people develop and utilize their talents in the service of others, created the wealth that funds non-profit and governmental activities, and provided products and services that have made our world a better place.

Business leaders and their engaged employees inspire us to grow in our character, competence, and contributions. Thank you!

TABLE OF CONTENTS

The Fourth Practice

INTRODUCTION

MIEDEMA COMPANIES IS A MARKETPLACE LEADER providing traditional and online auctions, as well as business liquidation services. Before their team got on the same page:

- Employees were disengaged
- Revenue growth was stagnant
- Profits were minimal
- The owners had become disenchanted

Now, they are on the same page. Within two years, the company experienced a dramatic turnaround.

- Employee engagement had measurably improved
- Revenues were up by more than 50%
- Profits had increased dramatically (and were being shared with the employees)
- The owners were delighted with the progress and their promising future

Over the past 25 years, we have been working with business owners and business leaders who want to develop higher performing organizations. Our clients include small and medium-size companies plus a few Fortune 500's from a wide range of industries—hospitality, engineering, utilities, technology, banking, construction, energy, financial services—you get the idea. A growing number of these companies have increased their revenues by 50% or more by implementing

PriorityAdvantage™. This book will help you understand and apply this proven methodology.

Herb Kelleher led Southwest Airlines to become America's highest performing company in one of the most challenging industries. With a focus on employee engagement, customer service, bottom line results, and leadership development, Southwest is one model of effective leadership.

"I don't really believe in, or pay much attention to, the folks who say that there's no work ethic in America today," Herb said. "But, they are driven, they are motivated, they are inspired by different things than people used to be. So, you have to be aware of that."

People want the kind of leadership that engages their individual strengths, brings people together, and accomplishes meaningful results.

PriorityAdvantage™ is comprised of four distinct leadership practices that have been developed in the crucible of growing, entrepreneurial businesses. These practices have been refined over time as our clients have helped us discover what really works to engage people and grow revenue and profits.

These four leadership practices get everyone on the same page and keep them there.

Though some of these leadership practices may appear obvious, by putting them to use, you'll learn how to get the most practical benefit. A few of them may also be unfamiliar, but when applied, we believe you'll find that you're able to save time, money, and frustration. You'll also benefit from increased communication, effectiveness, and profitability.

Here's the system in brief:

PRACTICES	COMPONENTS	SUMMARY
Practice 1 **PriorityPrinciples™**	Seven Ideas That Engage Employees and Accelerate Growth	Learn how to implement the principles that govern effective planning, achievement, and renewal.
Practice 2 **PriorityPlanning™**	Six Elements of a Dynamic Business Growth Plan	Learn how to write the six essential elements of a Dynamic Business Growth Plan.
Practice 3 **PriorityAchievement™**	Six Keys to Higher Achievement	Now it's time for action and results. Learn the essential leadership skills to make progress with your plan.
Practice 4 **PriorityRenewal™**	Five Accelerators of Renewal	Discover how to celebrate progress, learn from your experience, and adapt your course as you move forward.

Here is the big idea: what you're going to get here is not just business planning, but a leadership system. You'll learn how to refine your plan, increase your achievements, and keep everyone motivated to move forward as your business continues to do its day-to-day work.

You'll be able to learn this system in the next hour or so as you read through this book. However, mastery of this system—like any good

> *That executives give neither sufficient time nor sufficient thought to the future is a universal complaint.*
> —Peter Drucker
> The Father of Modern Management

habit—may take some time. Persist. While the short-term results can be impressive, there are even better results ahead when these practices become a habit. Why?

- You'll have a system for leading your business.
- You'll be organizing all the work required to achieve your vision.
- Your decision making will improve because the direction and priorities are clear.
- You can respond more rapidly to changing conditions.
- Your customers will receive better service.
- Your employees will be more engaged.
- Your business will be more productive and profitable!

THE FIRST PRACTICE:
PriorityPrinciples™

"It is our philosophical set of the sail that determines the course of our lives. To change our current direction, we have to change our philosophy, not our circumstances."
—Jim Rohn, Business Philosopher

WITHOUT UNDERSTANDING HOW THE WORLD of business works—what rules actually govern true business success—it's hard to make your way forward. It's like trying to sail a boat straight into the wind—you won't make much progress. But, once you understand and apply the PriorityPrinciples™, you learn how to jibe and tack, using angles to move upwind. Sailing becomes a lot easier and a lot more fun, no matter which way the wind is blowing.

PriorityPrinciples™
SUMMARY

PriorityPrinciples™	Definition
#1: The World's Greatest Leadership Principle	You reap what you sow. As you give, you receive.
#2: No Involvement, No Commitment	Get your team involved in the planning process. They will be more committed to making it happen.
#3: Never Fear Being Simple	Complexity leads to confusion and chaos. Simplicity leads to clarity, effectiveness, and efficiency.
#4: There's No Sin in Synergy	People with complimentary strengths can work together to achieve better results.
#5: 80/20—Are You in Business or Busyness?	There is an imbalance between causes and effects. Focus on the vital few causes that will produce the best results.
#6: Progress, Not Perfection	Your plan will never be perfect, but you can still make great progress as you define and achieve priorities.
#7: Leadership Requires a System	Systems are foundational to long-term, predictable success.

1

PRINCIPLE # 1 :

The World's Greatest Leadership Principle

"Let us endeavor so to live that when we come to die even the undertaker will be sorry."
—Mark Twain, Humorist and Writer

IN 2003, DR. GREGG RAYMOND'S dental practice was struggling. Revenues were at an all-time low. Turnover was at an all-time high. The demands of managing the business had become overwhelming. Gregg seemed to be at the end of his rope.

Gregg is a highly competent and compassionate cosmetic and family dentist. He is in the top 2% of his field and has the education, credentials, awards, and satisfied clients to prove it. Still, it's one thing to be a great dentist; it's another thing to build a great dental

> *Always do your best.*
> *What you plant now, you will harvest later.*
> —Og Mandino, Author

practice. Providing high quality products and services is no guarantee that any business will succeed.

Gregg decided it was time to reinvent his practice. He said, "The most significant thing that occurred was a foundational shift in my attitude." In the simplest of terms, Gregg and his team made it a priority to *give*.

- Gregg gave his team a listening ear and involved them in creating a dynamic business growth plan.
- Gregg gave his team generous profit sharing incentives.
- The team gave their best efforts to serving their customers and building a profitable business.
- The company gave free services to needy patients.

They gave and they received. Within two years, the business doubled their revenues, eliminated turnover, and infused a new spirit throughout the organization. Gregg and his team are fulfilling their mission statement, "Changing lives…a smile at a time…"

In our experience, any business can improve its people, productivity, and profits by

> *When businesses obsessively focus on serving customers, employees, and owners while fostering leadership throughout the organization, they are 756 times more profitable.*
> —John Kotter & James Heskett

applying the world's greatest leadership principle. The principle is counterintuitive. It doesn't make sense to some. They might suggest, "When you want to get more, go take it." No! When you want more, give more.

A study reported in Corporate Culture and Performance by John Kotter and James Heskett, points out that "firms with cultures that

> *Try not to become a person of success, but rather a person of value.*
> —Albert Einstein
> Nobel Prize-Winning Physicist

emphasized all the key managerial constituencies (customers, stockholders, and employees) and leadership from managers at all levels outperformed firms that did not have those cultural traits by a huge margin." They "improved their net incomes by 756 percent verses 1 percent."

2

Principle #2:
No Involvement,
No Commitment

"Men often oppose a thing merely because they have had no agency
in planning it, or because it may have been planned
by those whom they dislike."
—Alexander Hamilton
First Secretary of the Treasury of the United States

LET'S START WITH WHAT this principle is *not*. It's not about having everyone set the direction of the company. However, having people participate is absolutely essential for the creation of your plan and its execution. In our experience, the best visions do not come from groups; they come from inspired individuals who envision a better future. Therefore, *achieving* those visions comes easier when people are engaged in the visioning process.

Mary Kay Ash, the founder of Mary Kay Cosmetics, believed that when you ask for people's opinions, you make them feel important and help them buy into the plan. "People will support that which they help create. When you dictate even the most thoughtful and logical concept to a person—this idea is still a command. When you ask her to contribute to its inception, that very same idea becomes a personal crusade."

In 2003, George Marx knew that Copiah Bank could perform at higher levels, and he committed to lead the charge. The small community bank with six offices in central Mississippi had experienced very nominal growth over a ten year period. Then they increased in size by 53% in the next five years, enjoying measurable increases in assets, deposits, loans, and profits. More customers are being served, more employees are engaged, and the ownership is obviously pleased with their financial performance.

What happened?

George's first step was to work with his Board of Directors and get them on the same page by creating a Dynamic Business Growth Plan. Out of that initial meeting, a vision for growth, quality, and profitability emerged. George then convened his twelve key leaders who further developed their plan. These leaders then discussed the plan with every one of the 50 employees of Copiah Bank. George recently told us, "The PriorityAdvantage™ System provided us with direction, measurements, and a sense of accomplishment. The process has sparked enthusiasm, motivation, and ownership throughout the organization."

> *No executive has ever suffered because his subordinates were strong and effective.*
> —Peter Drucker
> Father of Modern Management

George successfully orchestrated a series of meetings that brought his entire team together with a shared sense of unity and purpose. By involving the stakeholders of Copiah Bank in the planning process, they were more committed to making the plan a reality.

What we're saying is this: there is a place for leadership and there is a place for teamwork. Leadership sets the course; teamwork figures out the best way to get there.

Companies can get this mixed up. If you have too much teamwork in creating a vision, it gets watered down. If you have too much leadership in implementation, you get chaos and micromanagement. Leadership needs to set the course and then step back and empower people to achieve results. However, your people must be involved in order to gain their commitment. Interestingly, we've often seen managers somewhat surprised when this happens. Their people often identify the same issues, projects, and processes as the managers. But here's the difference between involving and not involving your people in the planning: when people help define the issues, they're committed to

> *No involvement, no commitment.*
> —Stephen R. Covey
> Author and Educator

doing something about it. When management does all the defining, the people adopt a compliant attitude: "Just tell me what to do." Compliance starts a degenerating cycle where managers tend to dictate more, leading again to more compliance.

We agree with Herb Kelleher, Founder and Chairman Emeritus of Southwest Airlines, most people have a solid work ethic and are driven to achieve. They want to be involved.

3

PRINCIPLE #3:

Never Fear Being Simple

"You can't believe how hard it is for people to be simple, how much they fear being simple. They worry that if they're simple, people will think they're simple-minded. In reality, of course, it's just the reverse."
—Jack Welch, Chairman and CEO
General Electric

GLOBAL POSITIONING SATELLITE TECHNOLOGY is an amazing invention. If you have this in your car, you need only key in your destination, and a voice will direct you along the way. You will also receive written instructions.

Hemisphere GPS is a company that dominates the agricultural industry with GPS technology, and is making significant headway into technology for ships and airplanes.

In 2006, the Hemisphere GPS Board of Directors and Executives created a Dynamic Business Growth Plan. Although they work in a complicated, high-tech industry, the plan was clear and simple. Shortly thereafter, they shared their plan with a group of analysts from the Canadian Stock Exchange. The clarity and simplicity of the plan and the company's execution so excited the analysts that they began recommending the stock. The stock doubled in less than a year. Rick Heiniger, Vice-Chairman of Hemisphere GPS, said, "The ability to communicate a concise vision and strategy had a powerful impact on all of our stakeholders—leaders, associates, vendors, and investors."

The clarity and simplicity achieved in the plan had the greatest impact on people

> *Simplicity is the badge of genius.*
> —A. A. Montapert, Author

inside the organization. Rick went on to say, "The culture today is much, much different. It's one of collaboration, it's one of contribution, and it's one of engagement."

Today's world is growing increasingly complex. People are bombarded with so much information that they are losing their sense of confidence and capability. They wonder where they're going and if they have what it takes to get there. Good leadership starts with clear and simple communication.

To confirm clarity and simplicity, ask others to verbalize their understanding. If they can recite it back to you, you're doing well. If they can't, try communicating again. Remember always: keep it clear, keep it simple.

4

PRINCIPLE #4:
There's No Sin in Synergy

*"Entrepreneurs are marked by the ability to paint a
vision... managers tend to be more 'down to earth.' Their work
translates the visions of the entrepreneur into... performance.
Entrepreneurial and managerial talents must be brought within a
single harness if an organization is to succeed over time in a
rapidly changing environment."*
—James M. Strock, Management Consultant

THE IDEA THAT A LEADER CAN or should do it all is fading. It's
being replaced by what actually works in organizations: many talented
people working together, each contributing their unique strengths to the
enterprise.

We've discovered that many organizations have two distinctive types
of leaders. We call them Visionary Leaders and Operational Leaders.
When these two styles work together, organizations and their people

thrive. They achieve direction and clarity from the Visionary Leaders and effectiveness and efficiency from the Operational Leaders. By working together, they produce dramatically better results than they could by working separately. 1+1 can produce millions. That's called synergy.

In 1994, Michael Dell was feeling a bit overwhelmed. The wildly successful entrepreneur needed some help managing his growing business. So, he brought in Mort Topfer, a Motorola

> *You've got to know what you're good at because those are the cards you bring to the party. In other words, you need a sense of who you are and where you are going in order to be a successful manager.*
> —Larry Bossidy, CEO
> AlliedSignal

executive, who was known for his operational expertise. While Dell was working with customers on product development, giving speeches, and meeting with the press, Topfer focused on the day-to-day operations. During the next five years Dell sales grew at 48% annually and profits grew at 91% annually.

It's not always easy to get these two types of leaders to work together. Sometimes these two styles can come into conflict, and that conflict can hinder progress. The consequences of getting this dynamic right are huge. So let's examine how these two powerful and necessary styles can work together.

People on the visionary side have great insight into the marketplace. They work well outside the organization, bringing their vision of serving

> *Managers do things right.*
> *Leaders do the right things.*
> —Warren Bennis & Burt Nanus
> Authors

the marketplace back to their organization. They see what will benefit customers and they are persuasive at enrolling others in their vision. They can also get frustrated with procedures, forms, meetings, and systems. They often feel that the company isn't flexible enough, particularly when it comes to meeting the needs of the customer.

People on the operational side are strong at organizing and delegating work. They like to set up effective and efficient systems to increase quality and decrease costs and frustrations—all critical issues inside the organization. They may get frustrated with constant change, projects that get started but not finished, and a company's inability to get things organized and working efficiently.

Highly successful companies need both kinds of leaders to lead. They respect the visionary leaders for their insight into customers and their resistance to letting the company become too bureaucratic. They respect the operational leaders for bringing order out of chaos, saving costs, and running highly productive and efficient teams and systems.

So partner up. Your results are at stake!

5

PRINCIPLE #5:
80/20–Are You in Business or Busyness?

"Besides the noble art of getting things done, there is the noble art of leaving things undone. The wisdom of life consists in the elimination of nonessentials."
—Lin Yu Tang, Author

YOU'RE PROBABLY FAMILIAR with this principle. 80% of your profits come from 20% of your clients. 80% of your sales come from 20% of your product line. You wear 20% of your clothes 80% of the time. 20% of your relatives give you 80% of your heartaches.

It's not always exactly 80/20. Less than 5% of movies earn 97% of the revenue.

The point is that causes and effects are not equally distributed. A few causes have major impact, while most do not.

The 80/20 Principle has tremendous implications for the future of your business. We know you're busy. The question is, what are you busy about? Busyness, without focus, is bad business.

What are the few high-leverage activities that make the greatest impact on your organization's productivity and profitability?

> *The 80/20 Principle applied to business has one key theme—to generate the most money with the least expenditure of assets and effort.*
> —Richard Koch, Author

Three researchers studied this question. William Joyce, Nitin Nohria, and Bruce Roberson studied over 220 practices that have been advocated in leading business books in the last 25 years. (No wonder leaders are so confused!)

According to their book, <u>What Really Works: The 4+2 Formula for Sustained Business Success</u>, only eight of the 220 practices are high-leverage. The most important practice was to have a clear strategy.

Another primary practice was a rigorous discipline of achievement. PriorityPlanning™ and PriorityAchievement™ are 80/20 practices. In our experience, you will make more progress and achieve more results from forming habits around clear, effective planning and rigorous achievement, than around anything else you could do.

As you plan for your future growth, what 20% of your activities will provide 80% of your results?

In other words, where do you need to focus and what can you eliminate? In your business, there are many things you can probably reduce or stop doing altogether.

If you want to get a lot of fruit from a fruit tree, you must prune the branches. Too many blossoms produce many small fruits. To get big fruit, you must prune.

Without the practice of pruning, businesses develop the habit of just piling it on. When people don't get to everything they're "supposed to," they carry guilt and negative emotional baggage, worrying about it and regretting it. If you have people like this on your team, go through their activities with them and give them permission to stop doing the less important things. They're not getting to many of them anyway. At least you can take the emotional drag out of their lives.

One of the biggest barriers to high performance is the inability or unwillingness of owners to prioritize. They just insist that it must all be done. So they stay inefficient. They're not clear about what's really important, and they do not develop the corporate habit of rigorous execution. They can't bear much fruit because they're too busy trying to do too many things.

A business owner in the coffee shop business was a creative, intelligent, dynamic business leader. He had developed a great concept in a competitive market. In his creative moments, he could think of dozens of improvements the business needed to make.

Unfortunately, his staff couldn't execute all of his ideas. When they asked him to help them prioritize, he refused. "It's all important; just get it done," was his reply. You can imagine the results: chaos, pressure, disappointment, and stalled growth.

> *Those who analyze the reasons for their success know the 80/20 rule applies. Eighty percent of their growth, profitability, and satisfaction comes from 20 percent of their clients."*
> —Vin Manaktala, Author

Consistent application of the 80/20 Principle is foundational to accelerating growth and achieving long-term success.

6

PRINCIPLE #6:
Progress,
Not Perfection

*"I am careful not to confuse excellence with perfection. Excellence, I can
reach for; perfection is God's business."*
—Michael J. Fox, Actor

WHEN PLANNING, YOU MAKE decisions that have long-term consequences. It's natural to want to get it right the first time. The problem is, you can't always get it 100% right. Imagine you have a plan to drive across town. In theory, the plan may be perfect. However, once you start driving, variables like road construction or traffic conditions may dictate a change of plan. Investing too much time trying to achieve planning perfection for your business actually wastes time.

Here's the way through this quagmire: realize that you're in an *iterative* process. An iterative process means that you keep coming back to it in order to make it better. So, you don't have to be completely right the first time. You only need to be "good enough for now." Then, as you move forward, you can refine your plan.

We've found that this approach helps leadership teams move past the impossible standard of "perfect" in this work of planning. The goal for perfection may be commendable but, in practice, it is ultimately frustrating. It's frustrating because we can't know for sure what's going to happen. So, let's do the best we can for now, and then look at it again in the future.

Several years ago, we were invited to speak to a group of Forestry Association executives. One of those executives was Bruce Alt from the Mississippi

> *The cost of perfection will drive you out of business. What you are striving for is magic, not perfection.*
> —Michael Eisner, Chairman & CEO
> Walt Disney Productions

Forestry Association. Bruce and MFA's leadership continue to refine their Strategic Plan. The plan is becoming more clear and concise (and more widely understood by their members). Even though the first plan did not include "perfect verbiage," Bruce and his team at MFA were still able to define strategies and make meaningful progress on their 80/20 issues—membership, government affairs, and revenue.

Bruce recently said, "As an Association Executive, what I'm looking to create is forward momentum. That is the art of focusing a group of volunteer leaders on a consensus plan for achieving success. We can't allow one person, as well intentioned as they may be, to hijack the association and disrupt progress. Our planning creates continuity with leadership that changes every year. We build momentum as the planning and achievement cycle constantly improves."

So, seek progress without the expectation of getting it perfect. In that way, you'll get better without feeling like a failure. It's more natural, and it's a healthier way to do business.

The PriorityAdvantage™ System of planning, achieving, and renewing demonstrates this

> *There must be consistency in direction.*
> —W. Edwards Deming
> Author, Lecturer, and Consultant

principle. With each cycle, you get a little better. You learn some, apply it, learn some more, and get better. You get better at planning, achieving, and celebrating.

Then you get better at getting better.

We come back to finding the right balance. You want to get it right and you want to get it going. So, you do a little of each, strive to make it better, and be patient with yourself for what you've not learned yet.

7

PRINCIPLE #7:

Leadership Requires a System

*"If you can't describe what you are doing as a (system),
you don't know what you're doing."*
—W. Edwards Deming
"Father of the Japanese Post-War Industrial Revolution"

IN 1988, MICHAEL DREVER GOT INTO the vacation cruise business with $2,000 in cash and a $3,000 credit card loan. Who would have thought, that 20 years later, he would lead a business that included 105 locations and $300 million in revenue?

Rather unbelievable when we find out that Michael began his cruise industry career as a franchisee with a company that eventually went bankrupt. Michael bought that company out of bankruptcy and went on to create CruiseShipCenters, one of Canada's great business success stories. Michael said that after he bought the failed company, he realized that to become a successful franchisor, he must develop systems that would help the franchisees succeed. "I needed to work *on* the business, not just *in* the business," he said. Michael spent the first year developing integrated, documented, functional systems for the core elements of his business— Sales and Marketing, Administration, Operations, and Education.

When we met Michael, he adopted our methodology to simplify their planning system for the franchisees as well as the corporation. Michael said, "I've always run my life and business based on priorities. Finding PriorityAdvantage™ gave us a simple system to help our franchise partners, associates, and customers achieve their dreams."

In 1950, W. Edwards Deming, an American, began giving lectures to Japan's corporate leaders. Deming revolutionized business in

> *A system must have an aim.*
> *Without the aim, there is no system.*
> —W. Edwards Deming
> Author, Lecturer, and Consultant

Japan (and in the world) by helping organizations improve their systems. Companies such as Toyota, Sony, and Honda became symbols of quality.

His message was simple and profound, "Help people feel secure in their jobs, build quality that leads to lower costs, and most importantly— eliminate the defects that are caused by the system."

Thirty years later, in 1980, NBC News aired a television special called, "If Japan Can, Why Can't We?" Deming finally had an audience in his own country. Ford, for one, adopted a new mission statement in 1983, "Quality is Job 1."

Systems lead to higher productivity, lower costs, higher profits, greater company value, and greater security for everyone in the company.

> *Learning is not compulsory…*
> *neither is survival.*
> —W. Edwards Deming
> College Professor & Statistician

Leadership requires a system, and that system is planning, achieving, and renewing, based on principles.

THE SECOND PRACTICE:
PriorityPlanning™

"Having an effective growth planning system is the best indicator of whether your company will grow."
—Steven S. Little, Author

START BY CREATING A DYNAMIC BUSINESS Growth Plan, a roadmap for your success. The plan is clear and simple. It fits on a single page. It's easy to communicate to others. For most businesses, this happens first when they see the need to get on the same page. After that, it's often coordinated to fit with their fiscal year. The plan gives you a track to run on. It helps you organize the work of all your people so they're working toward the same end, and it gives you a way to measure your progress.

PriorityPlanning™
SUMMARY

TIME FRAME	SIX ELEMENTS	DYNAMIC BUSINESS GROWTH PLAN
LONG TERM 5-25 Years	**Vision**	***Where are we going?*** • What is our ideal future? • What will we provide to whom, and on what type of scale? • Is it clear and inspiring?
	Mission	***What's our purpose?*** • Does it explain why we do what we do? • Will it fit on a T-shirt?
	Values	***What will guide our conduct and decisions?*** • Do they arouse our highest degree of effort, proficiency, and character?
MID TERM 1-3 Years	**Objectives**	***How will we measure progress?*** • What are our key measures? • Are we measuring customer satisfaction, employee satisfaction, and financial success? • Are they clear and simple?
	Strategies	***How will we get to our vision?*** • What paths will we take? • What are the categories we will use to organize action? (For example: marketing, innovation, human resources)
SHORT TERM 90 Days or Less	**Priorities**	***Who will do what by when?*** • Do priorities connect to strategies? Is each priority assigned to a single individual? Do they define clear results?

8

ELEMENT #1:
Vision—
The End Comes First

*"You're not here merely to make a living. You're here to enable the
world to live more amply, with greater vision, and
with a finer spirit of hope and achievement.
You are here to enrich the world."*
—Woodrow Wilson
28th President of the United States

HOW DO YOU START implementing PriorityAdvantage™? You start
by creating a plan, and that starts by clarifying your vision.

The term 'vision' is related to the term 'visual'. So, one way to get at
vision is to create a clear picture. Describe for yourself in detail what your
company looks like five to twenty-five years from now. That is your vision.

During a recent meeting, Joe Wilson, President of Wilson Auctioneers,
leaned back in his chair, looked to the ceiling, and after a long pause
declared an inspired vision to his team. "You know what I really want us to

become?" he asked. "I want us to be the finest real estate auctioneers in Arkansas." This is Joe's passion. It played to his strengths, and it provided value to his marketplace. The entire team resonated with Joe's vision. Then Joe involved his team in creating and achieving a detailed plan to make that vision a reality. In the next year, the team at Wilson Auctioneers in Hot Springs, Arkansas doubled their revenues.

One way to evaluate a vision is to ask if it inspires. Do you feel it pulling you forward, describing a future that is worth the work and sacrifice you're going to be making?

> *Good business leaders create a vision, articulate the vision, passionately own the vision, and relentlessly drive it to completion.*
> —Jack Welch, Chairman & CEO General Electric

To keep the planning process simple, avoid trying to determine how the elements of your plan may sound to your prospects and customers. While that is a critical consideration for marketing, accommodating that concern now makes planning more difficult. So, when writing your plan, don't worry about how your vision will appear to all of your stakeholders. Instead, focus on getting just the people in your organization on the same page.

Consider these questions when clarifying your vision:

- What business are you in?
- Who are your customers?
- What are their needs?
- What products and/or services do you provide?
- How big do you intend to be?
- What will make you special in your marketplace?

There are many ways to write a vision. If you're stuck, here's a framework to get you started:

HOW TO CREATE AN INITIAL DRAFT OF YOUR VISION	
Inspiring picture of your position in your marketplace:	"The leading provider of
Products & Services:	residential fencing
Customers & Markets:	to homeowners
Scope:	in the metro area."

That's your vision: "We are the leading provider of residential fencing to homeowners in the metro area."

> *"Where there is no vision, the people perish."*
> Solomon
> King of Israel 971-931 BC

Once the vision is clear and shared by your team, you may want to choose more compelling language. For example, "San Diego's leading provider of residential fencing." Be patient with this iterative process. Inspiration can't be scheduled as a "to do" item in your planner.

If you put your vision into this format, you will have a clear and simple way to share it with others.

A vision can expand over time as your company grows.

When Meg Whitman served as eBay's Chief Executive, she was known for her vision and persistence. In ten years, eBay's revenue grew

> *The true motivator for employees is the spirit of cooperation that comes with a shared vision.*
> —Greg Bustin, Author

from $6 million to $7 billion. Their original vision was "to create the world's first global economic democracy." They envisioned a "people's market" in which anyone in the world could buy or sell anything for a fair price.

Now, the company has expanded their vision to, "Fostering the human connection through Social Commerce." Social Commerce is defined as, "a powerful combination of commerce, communication, and community that enhances traditional buying and selling."

Engaging employees and accelerating growth begins with a clear and compelling vision.

9

ELEMENT #2:
Mission–
The Power of Purpose

"A mission statement is defined as 'a long awkward sentence that demonstrates management's inability to think clearly.' All good companies have one."
—Scott Adams, The Dilbert Principle

MISSION IS PURPOSE. IT COMES FROM WITHIN. If vision inspires, mission motivates. If vision draws you, mission compels you.

Mission is that inner desire that seeks expression. It emerges from what drives us. Sometimes that may be a desire to serve, to create order, to provide value, or to give birth to beauty. In the business world, it is often expressed as the unique way in which you serve clients.

A mission works best when short. Peter Drucker says that a mission should fit on a T-shirt; it should be 10 words or less.

Defining their mission— their purpose—was a transformational experience for Dr. Steve Gradwohl and his team at Chiropractic

> *To love what you do and feel that it matters, how could anything be more fun?*
> —Katherine Graham, Publisher Washington Post

Treatment Center. They recently expanded their chiropractic and physical rehabilitation practice to include a focus on nutrition and enzyme therapy. Steve said, "We realized that our real purpose was not just about treating pain and illness. Our real mission is to provide 'Optimal Health for Every Patient.' So, we added new team members, purchased a new building, and expanded our marketing to better express our mission to the marketplace. We also changed our name to Optimal Health Center."

One landscaping company's mission is to "Create a more beautiful world." And they mean it! They create beautiful works of art in the outdoors using natural elements, especially those that grow.

The mission of Cruise Holidays of Kansas City is "Creating Memories that Last a Lifetime." Their clear purpose helped Mark and Mimi Comfort's team become the #1 franchise for 14 consecutive years.

Much of what we do every day is a means to an end. We drive our car to get somewhere; we exercise to maintain our health; we go to

> *Efforts and courage are not enough without purpose and direction.*
> —John F. Kennedy 35th President of the United States

work so we can pay the bills. But there are only a few things that we do just for the sake of doing them: serving others, creating beauty, learning, laughing, appreciating the creation, and worshipping the Creator. Mission often taps into one of these primary activities. We pursue our mission because the mission is worth doing on its own. The mission is an end, not a means to an end.

When you define vision, you go outward in your thought to the future. When you define your mission, you go inward into the heart of things, down deep to your central purpose.

> *"Here's the test to find whether your mission on Earth is finished: if you're alive, it isn't."*
> —Richard Bach, Author

In their book, Built to Last, Jim Collins and Jerry Porras suggest an effective way to define your mission. Simply ask the question, "Why not just shut this organization down, cash out, and sell off the assets?"

10

ELEMENT #3:
Values—
What's Right, Not
Who's Right

"A well-selected business value arouses people, calling for a high degree of effort, proficiency, or character. If it does not inspire, prod, or call to action, up the ante in the language you use."
—Rob Lebow & William L. Simon, <u>Lasting Change</u>

JACK WELCH IS WIDELY RECOGNIZED as one of the most effective business leaders of the 20th Century. Jack Welch's turnaround philosophy focused on speed, simplicity, and self-confidence. The 'GE Workout' concept empowered people to improve the organization. In his book, <u>Straight from the Gut</u>, he describes the significant role of values in transforming General Electric. GE's foundational value during their turnaround was a word that Jack created called "boundaryless."

32

The word 'boundaryless' is overflowing with meaning:

- Eliminating functional boundaries
- Breaking down walls of race and gender
- Sharing good ideas and the credit for developing them
- Learning from other companies

It's all about "Finding a Better Way Every Day." GE was creating momentum to become a high trust, high performing organization.

The values came to life at GE when Jack removed five high level managers for their lack of 'boundaryless' behavior. Results improved dramatically from that time forward.

An appropriate set of values provides a code of conduct that governs human behavior. Values define what is acceptable and not acceptable in the way we treat one another. Values build

> *You have to commit to values as you generate both personal and organizational energy. We spend so much time working: it's got to be fun as well as rewarding for people.*
> —Mike Armstrong, CEO
> AT&T

strong relationships and create high trust organizations. With a strong set of values, employees will often find greater acceptance, appreciation, and respect at work than in many other roles in their life.

McCown Gordon Construction has received numerous awards for the quality of their work and the speed of their growth. In 2005, 2006, and 2007, the Kansas City Business Journal honored their company as one of "The Best Places to Work in Kansas City." That award is primarily the result of three strongly held values. Pat McCown, CEO, puts it this way, "Some companies display their values on the walls of conference rooms, and others may choose to talk about them. At McCown Gordon, our values of 'Integrity, Relationships, and Performance' shine through each team member and drive us to everything we achieve."

When you identify your values—usually three to seven in number—they should accurately reflect who you are and who you want to be as an organization.

There are a couple of ways you can express your values. You can articulate your values as a phrase: "Dedicated professionals taking the initiative to serve with integrity and a positive attitude while treating others as we want to be treated." (Copiah Bank)

Or you can list values. The values of Marriott's Timber Lodge are: "Integrity, Accountability, Teamwork, Compassion, Fun, and Life/Work Balance."

Tom Cox and his team at Marriott's Timber Lodge also use a clarifying statement after each one of these six values.

Integrity	Consistent, honest, and ethical behavior creating trust and mutual respect.
Accountability	Commitment to "own it" and take personal responsibility insuring our actions equal our words.
Teamwork	Reaching beyond our roles to support and collaborate through a positive, energetic attitude to achieve shared goals.
Compassion	Seeking first to understand by engaging each other with caring, unconditional love, empathy, and sincere friendship.
Fun	Embodied by memorable celebrations, contagious enthusiasm, and a sense of humor.
Life/Work Balance	Maintained through self awareness of needs and appropriate managing of time and stress to achieve a healthy lifestyle.

A quick summary. Vision describes where you're going. Mission articulates why you're going there. Values define who you are at your core, and

> *It's important if you're successful that you set an example for the people who work for you in the way that you conduct your life.*
> —Richard Branson, Chairman
> The Virgin Group

how you treat each other along the way. These first three elements don't change much over time.

Let's look at how vision, mission, and values work together.

Mike Stange is a 'Level Five Leader' (to use the term coined by Jim Collins in his book, <u>Good To Great</u>). As the General Manager of Sandestin Golf & Beach Resort, Mike's leadership was defined by his teachable spirit and personal humility. He listened and learned from those around him. He gave credit to others. His competitive drive was consistently focused on helping Sandestin succeed.

Getting 1,400 associates on the same page is not an easy task. So, Mike first aligned his Executive Team, then the managers. Then they

> *"There would be fewer arguments if more of us tried to determine what's right instead of who's right."*
> —Anonymous

led two groups of 700 associates in clarifying the resort's plan, including vision, mission, and values.

The result of Mike's leadership was a vision, mission, and values that were clear and compelling.

VISION	To be the Southeast's premier resort destination.
MISSION	To create memories for our guests and colleagues—again and again.
VALUES	A dedicated team serving with integrity, excellence, accountability, and The Golden Rule.

Printed on a small wallet-size plastic card, the aspirations became an effective leadership tool. Mike and his team consistently used these long-term aspirations when hiring, training, and developing their associates.

In 2004-2005, Sandestin and their region were hit with numerous hurricanes. Mike said, "Our team really came together and we were able to prosper during the adversity. During the tough times, our vision, mission, and values became a rally cry. They challenged us to keep the compass pointed in the right direction."

The result? Sandestin's team achieved their financial objectives in the midst of this challenging season—good testimony to the power of having your team on the same page.

> *A leadership skill that inspires confidence and trust can be expressed in a variety of ways. It doesn't have to be charismatic. It can be pretty low key. But it has to be there.*
> —Ray Gilmartin, CEO
> Merck

11

ELEMENT #4:
Objectives—
What Gets Measured,
Gets Done

"How would you like to attend a basketball game where no one kept score, or watch a golf tournament without knowing the players' standings? Not much point, is there? Not much fun either."
—Jerry Haney, Speaker & Author

WHEN SCOTT STANGER AND THE LEADERSHIP team in their family owned business came together to get on the same page, it was obvious that some people had lost hope. For seven years the company's revenues looked like a roller coaster.

> *"Management by objective works if you first think through your objectives. 90% of the time you haven't."*
> —Peter Drucker
> Father of Modern Management

The idea of consistently growing revenues at 10%-15% a year seemed unachievable to many of their leaders. Yet, a few small changes in their strategic plan produced huge results as revenues grew by 40% annually the next two years. To hear Scott tell the company's success story, he sounds like an Old Testament prophet taking his flock to the Promised Land. According to Scott, "We were intentional in our efforts to get greater clarity in the planning process, which helped us create measurable objectives that everyone understood and bought into. Working together to establish goals we all believed in allowed us to tap into something inside the human spirit. We looked inside ourselves and looked to one another and realized we had all the raw materials in place. We had what it took to consistently grow our business." The company's vision, mission, and values helped Scott's team make better decisions. The objectives provided specific goals that defined success in numerical terms.

Objectives are the numbers or measures that indicate your progress. Think of the dashboard in your car. It has a

> *If a man does not know what part he is steering for, no wind is favorable to him.*
> —Anonymous

speedometer, a temperature gauge, and a fuel gauge. It may also have some warning lights that only come on when something is wrong or out of tolerance.

Your business needs a dashboard, a set of indicators that tell you how your business is doing.

There are four steps to establishing a good set of objectives:

1. Determine what to measure. Keep it simple. Simple measures lead to simple, straightforward business operations. Complicated measures encourage low-value and costly operations.

2. Balance the needs of your stakeholders: customers, employees, and owners (the CEO of the business). Usually this takes form in customer satisfaction, employee engagement, and financial performance.

3. Build the mechanisms for measurement. You may need to take a survey or conduct focus groups to get a benchmark established. Be

patient and persistent. In our experience, even with small companies, it may take a couple months or a couple of years to establish a good system of measures.

4. <u>Set a standard to reach</u>. This is the true objective. For example, you find that your first employee engagement index measures 2.6 on a 4.0 scale. You might set an objective to raise that to 2.75. So you would naturally want to identify those factors that could most impact that objective and focus there (another use of the 80/20 Principle).

One more word on objectives. There are two types of objectives—those that measure *outputs* (i.e., number of sales calls) and those that measures *outcomes* (i.e., dollar amount sold).

> *The three most important things you need to measure in a business are customer satisfaction, employee satisfaction, and cash flow.*
> —Jack Welch, Chairman & CEO General Electric

Here are some examples:

CATEGORY	OUTPUTS (Activities)	OUTCOMES (Results)
Sales	Number of sales calls	Dollar amount sold
Client Service	Average talk time	% of customers that intend to repeat business
Training	Number of people trained	% productivity gained from implementing new practices
Hiring	Number of candidates interviewed using job description	Lowered turnover %

You generally have more control over outputs—the activities that you're engaged in—but your organization and the marketplace will judge you

> *Nothing can add more power to your life than concentrating all of your energies on a limited set of targets.*
> —Nido Qubein, President
> High Point University

on your outcomes. The marketplace doesn't really care what your activities are; it's more interested in what value you're creating. So, when setting objectives, use outcomes not outputs whenever possible.

12

ELEMENT #5:
Strategies–
The Essential Element
to Accelerate Growth

"Creating the future is more challenging than playing catch up, in that you have to create your own road map. The goal is not simply to benchmark a competitor's products and processes and imitate its methods, but to develop an independent point of view about tomorrow's opportunities and how to exploit them."
—Gary Hamel & C.K. Prahalad
<u>Competing For the Future</u>

LARRY GRILL IS THE VICE PRESIDENT of Corporate Services for Alabama Power. Larry's eight-person leadership team serves 65 managers and supervisors, who serve the 600-member Corporate Services staff. These 600 people serve Alabama Power's 6,000 employees, who in turn serve more than one million residential, commercial, and industrial customers.

Larry recently explained his leadership philosophy, "The further you go up the corporate chart, the greater your responsibility to serve

> *A satisfied customer is the best business strategy of all.*
> —Michael LeBoeuf
> Consultant & Author

others. Unfortunately, many leaders lose the ego battle and undermine their own effectiveness. Leadership is best described as servant leadership."

Leaders serve the employees who, in turn, serve the customers. This is a winning strategy for any business.

After Joe Wilson and his team defined their vision to become "the premier real estate auctioneers in the state of Arkansas," they analyzed their current realities. They considered a variety of issues, including the marketplace, their competition, growth opportunities, plus their internal strengths and weaknesses. The next question was obvious: "Given what we know about our situation, how do we best achieve our vision?" The answer to this question defined their strategy. Wilson Auctioneers decided to serve more and bigger customers by investing in television advertising. This bold strategy helped the company double their revenues in the next twelve months.

Strategies are the high-level choices you make that determine the course you're going to follow. Strategies are pathways. They answer the question, "How are you going to get from here to your vision?"

> *It's very difficult to lead today when people are not really participating in the decision. You won't be able to attract and retain great people if they don't feel like they are a part of the authorship of the strategy...*
> —Howard Schultz, Chairman & CEO
> Starbucks

Usually you will have between three and eight strategies. These strategies should encompass all of the work that needs to be going on in your organization. If you

> *"In strategy it is important to see distant things as if they were close and to take a distanced view of close things."*
> —Anonymous

find some work that doesn't align with a strategy, either you need to add a strategy to your list, or stop doing that work.

There are many ways to write strategies, but we've found a way that's simple, easy, and effective.

1. Create your strategic categories. They might be called marketing, human resources, innovation, etc.
2. Start with a verb to clearly define the "end in mind."
3. Use the words 'by' or 'through.'
4. Follow with your strategic choices.

Here is an example of how to create a well written strategy:

Strategic Category	Marketing
End in Mind	"Reposition Wilson Auctioneering
'by' or 'through'	through
Strategic Choices	television advertising, updated promotional materials, and new signage."

A former colleague used to tell us, "In God we trust, all others bring data." This is especially true when developing strategies. After clearly defining your vision (where you want to go), you will want to take a hard look at your current realities (where you are now). Good data obtained from a wide range of sources will help you face the brutal realities and make better strategic decisions.

In ten years, Fishnet Security grew revenues from $200,000 to $200,000,000. The founder, Gary Fish, recently commented on the value of utilizing data when developing strategies.

"Because our business is a people business, it is very important for them to know that they are well taken care of. So, we do yearly Employee Satisfaction Surveys. We take that data and then try to grow from that year over year. And…we've actually seen it work. We've seen the scores go up, even through acquisitions." Fishnet uses the Survey data to develop their strategies.

Below are some other examples of well-written strategies:

STRATEGIC CATEGORY	STRATEGY
Human Resources	Develop a high-performing team through effective hiring, training, coaching, and compensation.
Innovation	Create new, desirable products through market research, creative design, and short product introduction cycle time.
Marketing	Attract more customers through targeted direct marketing campaigns, public relations, and customer workshops.

We often find that one strategy is most important, therefore, it's helpful to list the strategies in their order of importance.

From these examples, you can see the strategic choices being made. Once you decide you're going to attract more customers through targeted direct marketing campaigns, public relations, and customer workshops, it becomes apparent that you have specific results to produce in those three areas. You will define those results in the next section on Priorities.

13

ELEMENT #6:

Priorities—
The Missing Element
of Most Plans

"The key is not to prioritize what's on your schedule,
but to schedule your priorities."
—Stephen R. Covey
Author and Educator

OVER THE YEARS, MANY OF OUR clients have used the PriorityPlanning™ process to define and achieve their professional and personal priorities. Go with us on this...

Imagine your personal vision is, "Enjoy a long, healthy life of rewarding relationships and meaningful contributions." One of your personal strategies may be, "Maintain physical health and vitality through cardiovascular exercise, strength training, nutrition, and rest."

Let's take this a little further. Let's say you have an objective, "Complete the Shawnee Mission Triathlon in 2⅓ hours or less."

At this point, you can have the best intentions in the world, but if you don't set (and achieve) some priorities, the Sunday morning Triathlon

> *Plans are only good intentions unless they immediately degenerate into hard work.*
> —Peter Drucker
> Father of Modern Management

is not going to happen. So, one of your priorities may be, "Cross-train five hours per week."

In the past three decades, we've seen hundreds of business plans. Many of them are lengthy documents sitting on a shelf collecting dust. Almost every one of those plans is missing the most important element— priorities, who is going to do what by when. Whereas, lengthy plans that sit on a shelf might be good for *borrowing money*, a Dynamic Business Growth Plan (with priorities) is better for *making money*.

Priorities are the key lynchpins in the planning process. While the first five elements of your plan are

> *Don't be a time manager, be a priority manager.*
> —Denis Waitley, Author

critical to clarifying direction (vision, mission, values, objectives, and strategies), priorities are critical to achievement. In other words, the accomplishment of priorities defines results. To master achievement is to master the skill of defining and accomplishing priorities.

A good priority describes an outcome or a result. A poor priority describes a routine, an action, or a start.

Here are some samples:

INEFFECTIVE PRIORITIES	EFFECTIVE PRIORITIES
Launch new direct mail campaign by March 31.	Achieve a 10% increase in direct marketing leads by March 31.
Research new products for next fiscal year.	Make new product recommendations to Leadership Team by November 12.
Send Jim to Consumer Products convention in December.	Debrief Consumer Products convention at our team meeting on January 31.

Do you see the problems in the left hand column? In some cases, the priorities are too vague. (How can you tell when you're finished with researching new products?) In other cases, the priority is not really the final result you want ("Send Jim to Consumer Products convention").

It's common for individuals to achieve dozens of additional priorities each year by using this approach. Imagine a team of 12 people, each accomplishing 36 additional priorities in a year. What impact would that have on your leadership development and organizational performance?

Here are five guidelines for writing Priorities:

1. <u>Start with a verb</u>. The best verbs show completed actions. "Finish," "complete," and "debrief" are better verbs than "launch," "study," "manage," or "help."

2. <u>End with a date</u>. To establish a high-achievement culture, you must be in the habit of putting dates on actions. Without a date, how can someone prioritize the action steps? How can you have accountability? The little habit of putting dates on agreements can literally, all by itself, transform a low-performing culture to a higher-performing culture.

3. <u>Make it measurable or observable</u>. Here's the question you need to ask: Can you tell when the priority is done? If not, it's not specific enough. You can tell if a priority that starts with "make recommendations" is finished. You can't if the priority starts with "study." If you can tell when it's completed, then you can also tell how much progress you've made. If there's no clear way to tell when you're complete, then you won't be able to tell how far along you are.

4. <u>Assign a priority to one person</u>. That doesn't mean one person does all the work. It means that one person is responsible for seeing that the work gets done.

> *Make service your first priority, not success, and success will follow.*
> —Anonymous

5. <u>Link every priority to a strategy</u>. This gives everyone a direct line of sight: my priority connects to a company strategy which connects to our vision. In other words, my work helps us achieve our vision.

VISION	To become the region's premier high-end bike retailer.
STRATEGY	Build a high performing team by hiring, training, managing, and compensating top talent.
PRIORITY	(Meg) Hire two sales reps to start work by September 15th.

The number one reason for poor performance is that people don't know what is expected of them. Setting clear priorities addresses this issue.

The number two reason for poor performance is that people don't know how they're doing—we don't track

> *"Establish your priorities and go to work."*
> —H. L. Hunt, Oil Tycoon

people's progress. We'll address that issue in the next section.

THE THIRD PRACTICE:
PriorityAchievement™

PriorityPlanning™

PriorityPrinciples™

PriorityRenewal™   **PriorityAchievement™**

"Effective leadership is not about making speeches or being liked; leadership is defined by results not attributes."
—Peter Drucker, Father of Modern Management

THIS IS THE DAY-TO-DAY DISCIPLINE of managing time to get your most important work done. Once you know what results your people are to produce (the Dynamic Business Growth Plan), you can track progress on your most important priorities. Whether people are achieving goals, solving problems, or building capacity, you can track how they're doing. Are they getting it done? Are they on time? Are they using the right amount of resources? Achievement gets you to your destination.

PriorityAchievement™
SUMMARY

PriorityAchievement™ Keys	Definition
#1: Prioritize!— Focus on Your Most Important Priorities	By focusing on achieving your most important priorities, you maximize personal and professional results.
#2: Define Action Steps— Action People, Action!	Create Action Steps. Take one step at a time. Enjoy the journey.
#3: Set Achievement Cycles— It's About Time!	High performing teams are strengthened as they set, achieve, and celebrate priorities in Achievement Cycles (usually four, six, or thirteen week time frames).
#4: Get "Unstuck"— The Power of a Next Step	Sometimes we get stuck. What do we do then? Managers and co-workers can help us move forward.
#5: Achieve Together— It's Great That You're Different	Different people with different strengths achieve different results in different ways.
#6: Be a Leader That Matters— The Wind in Their Sail!	The role of the manager is critical to high performance. Effective managers build strong relationships with employees and achieve better results.

14

Key #1:

Prioritize!– Focus on Your Most Important Priorities

"The way you spend your time is a result of the way you see your time and the way you really see your priorities."
—Stephen R. Covey, Author and Educator

AT ANY GIVEN TIME, YOU HAVE a couple dozen things that you could do. The 80/20 principle helps you identify your most important priorities. The 80/20 principle further helps you identify the single most important one. Start there and go to work.

Decades ago, management consultant Ivy Lee advised the CEO of Bethlehem Steel, Charles Schwab, to create a prioritized list of the most important tasks he needed to accomplish each day and then focus on achieving them one at a time. Schwab said it was the most profitable lesson he had ever learned and wrote Ivy Lee a check for $25,000.

So what are your most important tasks and priorities? How do you stay focused on what's most important to you?

> *Write down the most important tasks you have to do tomorrow, and number them in order of importance.*
> —Ivy Lee to Charles Schwab

We often use a two-sided card that fits in a billfold with room to write your Top 5 Personal Priorities on one side and your Top 5 Professional Priorities on the other side.

TOP 5 PERSONAL PRIORITIES

1 _____
2 _____
3 _____
4 _____
5 _____

TOP 5 PROFESSIONAL PRIORITIES

1 _____
2 _____
3 _____
4 _____
5 _____

By defining personal and professional priorities in this way, it's easy to stay focused on what's most important.

Different people set and achieve priorities in wildly different ways. Some people are more structured, some are more random. Some people prefer putting things in writing, some don't. But the questions are always the same:

> *Time is an equal opportunity employer. Each human being has exactly the same number of hours and minutes every day. Success depends upon using it wisely by planning and setting priorities.*
> —Denis Waitley, Author

- Have you clarified what's most important?
- Are you making progress?

When we are asked to facilitate client workshops, we use "participant-centered learning" techniques. We have learned many of these principles and practices from the Bob Pike Group.

In the fall of 2005, Bob Pike asked us to help his team develop a Dynamic Business Growth Plan to engage employees and accelerate growth.

"Our first step," said Russ Lilienthal, COO of the Bob Pike Group, "was getting our team on the same page. It was clear from the workshop exercises that we all wanted the same things. It did take awhile", Russ continued, "to believe that we could achieve 20% annual growth."

"Then, we set and achieved high-leverage priorities that made a significant impact. The hardest thing was to keep the entrepreneurial dreamers

> *I've begun to realize that I can't have it all. I used to think that I could if I scheduled artfully enough. But you have to make choices.*
> —Joy Covey, Chief Strategy Officer Amazon.com

focused on what we needed to finish, before we added new priorities. By finishing what we started, our team achieved spectacular results—customer satisfaction improved, revenue per full-time equivalent grew by 25%, and we experienced no turnover."

Russ concluded, "Leadership was evident throughout our organization. Setting priorities made my job easier and we all had more fun!"

15

KEY #2:
Define Action Steps—
Action People, Action!

"He who every morning plans the transaction of the day and follows out that plan, carries a thread that will guide him through the maze of the most busy life. But, where no plan is laid, where the disposal of time is surrendered merely to the chance of incidents, chaos will soon reign."
—Victor Hugo, French Poet and Playwright

IT HAS BEEN SUGGESTED THAT one minute of planning time saves twelve minutes of execution time. The busier we are, professionally and personally, the more important it is to plan, prioritize, and define tasks.

Nor-son is a design/build construction service company headquartered in Brainerd, Minnesota. In three years, their revenues have grown from $36 million to $56 million.

Bob Sweeney, CEO, attributes their growth to "a culture that is embracing change, personal development, ongoing planning, and process improvement." One of those processes, PriorityAchievement™, helps Bob's team develop priorities with action plans.

Bob said, "Our people are bright and motivated. They want to make significant contributions. Action plans help us get the best results in the least amount of time."

> Setting a goal is not the main thing. It is deciding how you will go about achieving it and staying with that plan.
> —Tom Landry,
> Dallas Cowboys Football Coach

This is a useful and often overlooked practice. People don't execute priorities directly. Priorities are results. People execute or accomplish tasks. So to make the most progress—in the easiest and fastest way—you may want to create an Action Plan.

An Action Plan is a list of tasks needed to achieve a priority. Some of those tasks you'll do yourself and some you may delegate to others. However, no matter who is performing the task, an action plan is critical.

Here's an example:

PRIORITY: Hire Two Sales Reps by January 31st		
Name	*Action Plan*	*Date*
Marta	Gather candidate records by advertising or searching Monster or CareerBuilder.	Jan 4
Marta	Score candidate records by hiring criteria.	Jan 9
Shauna	Conduct screen interviews with remaining candidates.	Jan 15
Tracy	Interview final candidates.	Jan 22
Marta	Assess final candidates.	Jan 23
Marta	Complete background & reference checks.	Jan 25
Tracy	Make a decision, extend an offer.	Jan 28
Shauna	Contact remaining final candidates to inform them of the decision.	Jan 31

You have a *task* when you know who does what by when. Until then, all you have is a *wish*.

Action Plans reduce frustration and wasted energy. When you've accomplished one task, you move on to the next—no wasting time trying to define what the next task should be.

> *The more time we spend planning a project, the less time is required for it. Do not let today's busy work crowd planning time out of your schedule.*
> —Edwin Bliss, Author

Action Plans translate intentions into actions. They transform dreams into achievements.

A good Action Plan aligns managers and team members. It gets them on the same page. If an Action Plan is flawed, they can catch it before spending a lot of time and energy. They save the time it takes to do it wrong, and they save the time it takes to fix it.

Action Plans overcome hurdles to achievement. Often when a person gets stuck in accomplishing a priority, it's because one of two barriers have emerged:

> *Mechanical reminders are often very helpful to keep from getting enmeshed in the details of the day and losing sight of the specific things you must do to move toward your goal.*
> —Brownie Wise, Entreprenuer Tupperware

- They don't know what to do next
- The next task is too big

Action Plans help you prevent both barriers to achievement. They show you what to do next and they break the work up in small pieces.

16

KEY #3:

Set Achievement Cycles— It's About Time!

"Dost thou love life? Then do not squander time, for that is the stuff life is made of."
—Benjamin Franklin, Author, Inventor, and Statesman

AN ACHIEVEMENT CYCLE IS THE TIMEFRAME you utilize to set and achieve priorities. It's the period of time you choose to communicate and celebrate progress with your team.

What's the right time period for an Achievement Cycle? You'll want to choose a time frame that will work for your team. The Marketing and Sales teams within Marriott Vacation Clubs meet every four weeks. Most of our clients meet every month. Miedema Companies meets every quarter.

Within the achievement cycle, each person focuses on the tasks that help them achieve their most important

> *You will never find time for anything. If you want time you must make it!*
> —Charles Burton, Author

priorities. It's all about the effective use of time. So, schedule time during each achievement cycle to accomplish what matters most.

Here's an example of how Action Steps are scheduled and priorities are achieved:

ACTION STEPS (AS)

AS-1) Gather candidate records

AS-2) Score candidate records

AS-3) Conduct interviews

AS-4) Interview final candidates

AS-5) Assess final candidates

AS-6) Complete reference checks

AS-7) Extend offer

AS-8) Contact remaining candidates

SUN	MON	TUES	WED	THURS	FRI	SAT
		1 New Year's Day	2	3	4 AS-1	5
6	7	8	9 AS-2	10	11	12
13	14	15 AS-3	16	17	18	19
20	21 Martin Luther King Jr. Day	22 AS-4	23 AS-5	24	25 AS-6	26
27	28 AS-7	29	30	31 AS-8		

Nido Quebin is the President of High Point University. Nido utilizes a unique and productive system to manage his time. Nido and his team frequently divide

> *You can either take action or you can hang back and hope for a miracle. Miracles are great, but they are so unpredictable.*
> —Peter Drucker
> Father of Modern Management

hours into twelve five minute segments. Nido desires to do each task effectively and efficiently. In other words, he wants to get the maximum results with his time. Here are some examples of what Nido achieves in five minutes:

- Meet with the parents of a potential new student who are touring the campus with their child.
- Hold a stand-up meeting (to encourage people to get to the point).
- Compliment someone on a job well done.
- Communicate the organization's mission, vision, and values to a new employee.
- Leave phone messages for employees on their Birthday.
- Write brief responses to e-mails (like Nido's e-mail response that helped us write this segment).

As you can imagine, Nido is a very productive person. In addition to serving as a College President, he is also an author, professional speaker, entrepreneur, and philanthropist. Pretty amazing

> *The more you communicate with every associate, the better job they'll be able to do, the happier they'll be, and therefore, they'll be more productive.*
> —Ewing Kauffman, Founder
> Marion Labs

for a guy who arrived in America at 17 with $50 in his pocket.

Each of us has a unique opportunity to make significant contributions, and at the end of the achievement cycle, we should celebrate progress.

The idea of the achievement cycle, first came to us from Ewing Kauffman.

Ewing Marion Kauffman started Marion Labs in his basement in 1950 with $5,000. By the 1980's, he had become a billionaire and almost 10% of his associates had become millionaires.

Kauffman said, "At Marion, it is our intention to treat others as we would like to be treated—with dignity, respect, and integrity. We believe it and we live it."

Mr. K, as he was lovingly referred to by his associates, told us, "We have meetings four times a year with all the associates at Marion. One of our associates, whose husband is a partner in a corporate law firm downtown, went home and told him about the Marion Meeting; what we had done, what we were going to do in the next 30 days, 90 days, and one year. Her husband said, 'You know more about your company than I know about mine, and I'm a partner.' That's how well we communicate."

These meetings were called, "Marion on the Move." This approach will work with any organization. Achievement comes in cycles and people have a need to be updated on the plan and the progress.

17

KEY #4:

Get "Unstuck"– The Power of a Next Step

"A leader is someone who translates intention into reality and sustains it."
—Warren Bennis, Author

BY DEFINING PRIORITIES WITH action plans that align to your organization's most important strategies, any business can increase growth, productivity, and profitability.

We also know that achievement doesn't always go smoothly. People get stuck! Maybe our action plan skipped over an action step, maybe we needed information from a third party, or maybe someone else didn't finish their action step and you find yourself waiting. Whatever the case may be, people get stuck! The important thing to remember at these times is that you are not alone. Your manager and your co-workers can help. Other people want to help you get unstuck and get back on track.

To get unstuck, you define who is going to do what by when in order to get the priority back on track.

> *Our responsibility is to encourage and drive them to achieve, and help them where they fall short, so they can ultimately succeed.*
> —Chuck Knight, Chairman
> Emerson Electric

The life of Oprah Winfrey offers a dramatic example of getting unstuck. Oprah Winfrey was born to a single mom in 1954. At four years of age, she toured local churches reciting sermons that she had heard. She was raped at 9 and got pregnant at 13. Her baby was born prematurely, and died shortly after birth. A lesser person might have also let their dreams die. Not Oprah!

At 23, she had her own TV talk show and at 32, she was broadcasting nationally. In 2003, at the age of 49, Oprah was the first African-American woman to become a billionaire.

What happened? How did Oprah get unstuck?

After Oprah lost the child from her teenage pregnancy, her mother sent her to live with her father, Vernon Winfrey, a businessman in

> *"All grand strategies eventually deteriorate into work."*
> —Peter Drucker
> *Father of Modern Management*

Nashville, Tennessee. Vernon inspired his daughter with thoughts of a better future. He encouraged her to read biographies of famous people and study success literature. That's when Oprah decided to dedicate her life to helping people live better lives. From that time forward, everything was different.

Here are some less dramatic, more common, examples of people getting stuck, and their next steps.

Being Stuck	A Next Step
The next step is intimidating.	Break the next step up into smaller steps. Sometimes when you're climbing a mountain, the path isn't clear until you've climbed up the hill a bit. Then you can see what needs to be done. Move forward where you can.
I have to give someone bad news and I don't want to do that.	Write up your message and review it with someone that's good at giving bad news. Role play it with that person.
I don't know what the next step is.	Ask for help. Go to an experienced person and say, "Here's the situation I'm in. What do you see as some possible next steps?"
I'm waiting to get a decision from my boss.	Remind the boss—not that you're waiting—but what the consequences are of delay.

From time to time we all get stuck. We need help. In an organization, that's when managers and colleagues can come to the rescue.

If you don't understand that you should be working for your mislabeled "subordinates" you haven't understood anything. Lead yourself, lead your superiors, lead your peers, and free your people to do the same. All else is trivial.
—Dee Hock, Founder
VISA

18

KEY #5:

Achieve Together— It's Great That You're Different

"The essence of synergy is to value differences— to respect them, to build on strengths, to compensate for weaknesses."
—Stephen R. Covey, Author and Educator

KELLY SCHOEN IS THE CEO of an award-winning direct marketing company, Z3 Graphix. Z3 has a clear and compelling mission statement, "Helping our customers find more customers." Their strategies focus on building a high performing team, improving operational efficiency, and increasing revenues.

Kelly takes calculated risks. He creates urgency. He is futuristic and strategic. Kelly is a visionary leader with the accompanying achievement drive and restlessness that often clashes with more stable, consistent performers. That was exactly the case between Kelly and Denise.

Denise is Z3's Customer Service Manager. She has responsibility for implementing priorities relating to achieving high levels of customer satisfaction. Denise has a high capacity for detail and complexity. Denise is organized and naturally thinks in terms of higher levels of efficiency.

So, what was the problem? Kelly felt that Denise was resistant to the constant improvements and changes

> *Alone we can do so little;*
> *together we can do so much.*
> —Helen Keller, Activist and Author

that he wanted to make in the business. But, that was not the case at all! Denise was perfectly willing to go along with Kelly's plan as long as she was given enough details, and of course, she wanted the change to be structured and orderly.

With these kinds of differences (often found in leaders at the top levels in an organization), they had a choice. They could choose a path of synergy or a path of conflict.

As Denise and Kelly came to understand and appreciate their complimentary strengths, they chose the path of synergy. What they discovered was that Kelly preferred *creating* the Plan while Denise preferred *implementing* the Plan. Z3 Graphix needs both people because high performance requires both disciplines.

Kelly and Denise worked together with the executive team to get on the same page and achieve their priorities. The result? "In our first three months, we accomplished more than we had in the previous two years combined." Kelly said, "Every month our

> *What is the recipe for successful*
> *achievement? To my mind there are*
> *just four essentials:*
> *Choose a career you love…*
> *Give it the best there is in you…*
> *Seize your opportunities…*
> *And be a member of the team.*
> —Benjamin F. Fairless, President
> U.S. Steel

leadership team would meet to celebrate progress and set new priorities. The cycle of setting, achieving, and celebrating priorities on a monthly basis made all the difference." Denise recently reported achieving 47 high leverage priorities in 14 months.

Leadership synergy creates high achievement teams. Leaders work together and achieve more because of their differences.

> What I wanted was to be allowed to do the thing in the world that I did best, which I believed then and believe now, is the greatest privilege there is. When I did that success found me.
> —*Debbi Fields, Founder*
> *Mrs. Fields' Cookies*

19

KEY #6:

Be a Leader that Matters–The Wind in Their Sail!

"Coaching: To get people to do what they don't want to do in order to achieve what they want to achieve."
—Tom Landry, Dallas Cowboys Football Coach

ACCORDING TO A RECENT CONVERSATION with James Harter, Chief Scientist with The Gallup Organization, Gallup's research shows that 30% of the American workforce is engaged, 55% is disengaged, and 15% is actively disengaged. Engaged employees go the extra mile; they are "achievers". Disengaged employees put in their time; they are "coasters." Actively disengaged employees, according to James Harter, are "destroyers." They destroy their organization and the people that work in their organization.

Gallup Research Results			
Percentage of Workforce	Gallup's Employee Descriptor	Employee Behavior	Employee Label
30%	Engaged	Goes the extra mile	"Achievers"
55%	Disengaged	Puts in their time	"Coasters"
15%	Actively Disengaged	Destroys the organization and people around them	"Destroyers"

So, how do organizations engage employees? The role of the manager is critical. Here are some proven ways for managers to engage employees:

> *The job of the manager is enabling, not a directive job... Coaching and not direction is the first quality of leadership now. Get the barriers out of the way to let people do the things they do well.*
> —Robert Noyce, Founder Intel

- Connect people to the Mission, enabling people to see that their job is important.
- Help people understand what is expected of them by defining priorities and action plans.
- Recognize and praise people's progress and hold them accountable for their commitments.
- Help people identify, develop, and utilize their strengths.
- Respect people, their opinions, and their growth.

What happens if people haven't accomplished their priorities? This is critical. If you fumble here, it's hard to get momentum.

When you see that an expectation is not being met, you must say something. Not to say something is to make a loud pronouncement that it's O.K. to be satisfied with substandard performance.

To coach effectively: Ask questions to help people figure out what to do. Asking questions builds capacity. Telling people what to do destroys capacity. The following is one example of how questions enable the employee to re-engage their efforts and achieve results.

You	They
"Mike, your recommendations are late. This not what I expected from you."	"I know, and I'm not pleased myself. I'm working on it today."
"When can I expect to see it?"	"Monday morning, first thing."
"But I will need it Friday morning. Can you get it to my by then?"	"Yes, I can get it to you by Friday morning."
"What's your plan for completing it by then?"	"I will just be sure to get it done."
"Tell me what steps you'll take"	"I'll just work late."
"Who else can be involved to help you?"	"Well, I suppose Pat could help."
"Good. Who else might be able to help?"	"I'm going to need some help accessing some information on the server. I'll need Louise to help out."
"O.K. I'll call her and let her know to support you on this. What else?"	"I think that's it."
"O.K. Do you foresee any reason why you won't be able to make this new deadline?"	"No, I think that's it."
"Fine. I'll expect to see you at 9:00 on Friday morning in my office."	

When you expect a lot from your people, they may think you're unreasonable. Yet we've often seen managers make demands on people that appeared to be too high. These people found that they could rise to the occasion. Recall the 1980 US Olympic hockey team. Their coach, Herb Brooks, was unreasonable in his expectation that they could beat the Soviets. After all, they were amateurs from college teams and they had never played together before. The Soviets had dominated the Olympics since 1964. Yet the players went beyond themselves. They played the best team in the world—and beat them. They went on to win the gold medal.

> *A leader is someone who can take a group of people to a place they don't think they can go.*
> —Bob Eaton, Chairman and Co-CEO DaimlerChrysler

On the other hand, we've seen managers make demands that were so unreasonable they became completely ineffective. We know of one business that had a revolving door to handle the consistent turnover. The top person was demanding and critical.

Find the place where you get the balance right. Too soft and you lose results. Too hard and you lose people.

Let's go back to the person who's not meeting an expectation.

Your purpose here is to increase the capacity of your people. That means that they need to grow to be able to solve bigger, more complex problems. They need the physical, mental, and emotional capacity to produce greater and better results.

> *Holding people accountable helps them grow. People want to know if they haven't done a good job and how they can do better.*
> —Chuck Knight, Chairman Emerson

You must address substandard performance the first time it emerges. That's how you set expectations. Be calm, but firm. If you wait a day or two or five, you're sending a message that it's acceptable to be late a day or two or five.

To run a tighter ship, you need to follow-up on missed expectations immediately.

To summarize:

- Address the performance issue the first time it shows up.
- Coach people to increase their capacity. Do this by asking questions, not dictating answers.

THE FOURTH PRACTICE:
PriorityRenewal™

PriorityPlanning™

PriorityPrinciples™

PriorityRenewal™   PriorityAchievement™

"We want to be a company that is constantly renewing itself, shedding the past, adapting to change."
—Jack Welch, Chairman and CEO
General Electric

On a regular basis, your leadership team steps back from the day-to-day work to renew the people and the plan:

- What have your people achieved? Celebrate.

- What are your people learning? Share.

- What changes need to be made to the plan? Adapt.

- Who needs to do what by when? Commit.

PriorityRenewal™
SUMMARY:

PriorityRenewal™ Accelerators	Definitions
#1: The Spirit of Renewal	Renewing is consistently looking for ways to improve the plan and develop your people
#2: Celebrate Your People	Recognize your people and their achievements
#3: Learn From Your Experience	Tell the stories that increase everyone's effectiveness
#4: Evaluate Your Plan	Examine your plan and adapt it to your changing environment
#5: Commit to New Priorities	Based on where you are now, establish priorities for moving forward

20

ACCELERATOR #1:

The Spirit of Renewal

"Inside every old company is a new company
waiting to be born."
—Alvin Toffler, Author

JOE AND JERRY LAMBERT AND MARK MCWILLIAMS started their business in 1990. For the first six months, they didn't receive a paycheck. By the end of the first year, they grossed $600,000 in revenue with 5 employees. Today, United Heating, Cooling & Plumbing operates out of a 113,000 square foot building on 14 acres, with 250 employees, 170 trucks, and $25,000,000 in annual revenue.

Joe Lambert, President of United Heating, Cooling & Plumbing said, "PriorityAdvantage™ helped us get out of a funk. We weren't growing like we wanted and it seemed like the three owners were making all the decisions."

Joe went on to say, "Empowering our people has made our lives easier. We were working 12-14 hour days, 6-7 days a week. Three years later, our business has grown by 50%, and I usually work 8-10 hour days, 5 days a week. We empowered our people, and it has made all the difference."

Joe has uncommon stamina. He gets to the office at 5:45 a.m. daily. He delegates work and then does the things that only he can do. Joe is a visionary, and clearly sees the future they are building. United is building a system that could succeed in virtually any North American city.

Joe told us, "Here's the good news: we don't have to be here. We have enough capable people to run the business without us. We trust our people to do the right thing. We help our people succeed. We give them the tools, provide on-the-job training, and care about them as more than an employee. We help them deal with their issues, professionally and personally."

> *Hire the best. Pay them fairly. Communicate frequently. Provide challenges and rewards. Believe in them. Get out of their way and they'll knock your socks off.*
> —Mary Ann Allison, Vice President Citicorp

Joe believes that leadership is all about treating people with honesty and respect. From time to time, employees can't work because of a serious illness, injury, or a family crisis. In these times of need, co-workers give vacation days, or even cash, and the company matches their gifts. It's not uncommon for families to receive $5,000-$12,000. Joe believes in teaching people the joy of giving.

United has built their business by doing the right thing and developing a solid reputation. Their team comes together for a Weekly Renewal

> *We think profits are important, but they're not as important as the individual.*
> —Bill Marriott, Chairman Marriott International

Breakfast at 6:30 a.m. every Thursday morning to celebrate progress, communicate important information, and build relationships.

Before a recent slowdown in new construction, United implemented a strategy that would provide greater stability for the employees and their families. They decided to expand their service and replacement business, as well as their commercial business.

Joe concludes, "We've always tried to improve on the way we do our work. We're reinventing our business about every three months. Then, our competition copies us and we find new and better ways to improve ourselves again."

That's the spirit of PriorityRenewal™. Renew the plan; renew the people.

21

ACCELERATOR #2:

Celebrate Your People

"Always treat your employees exactly as you want them to treat your best customers."
—Stephen R. Covey, Author and Educator

PEOPLE, IN NEARLY EVERY COMPANY that we work with, tell us that they do not invest enough time and effort recognizing people's contributions. Too often we work, work, work, and then we work some more. PriorityRenewal™ is an opportunity to recognize your people and their progress. This helps people consistently engage their best efforts while avoiding burn-out.

When Jim Manley was serving as Vice President of Human Resources for Intercontinental Hotels, he told us, "Most people underestimate the positive impact of celebration. Of course, people need vision, strategies, and priorities to move forward. We

> *Celebrate what you want to see more of.*
> —Tom Peters, Author

also need to celebrate people's progress. Recognition further develops the person—the organization's most important asset."

Many business leaders do not realize the power they have to frame the positive experiences and culture of their company. If you call attention to a person or a team as having accomplished something significant, it becomes significant. To a great extent, you define what is important by how you feel about it, and what you say about it.

It's easy to celebrate progress. For many individuals, you need only say something about someone's accomplishment, but be sure to make it a big deal! By acknowledging a contribution, you honor that person, their efforts, and their results.

Mary Kay Ash said, "I never yet met a person who didn't want to be appreciated." At Mary Kay, Ash set up a recognition system ranging

> *Treat people as if they were what they ought to be, and you may help them to become what they are capable of being.*
> —Johann Goethe, Author

from a simple "thank you for showing up early" to a pink Cadillac. Ash wrote, "We go first class, and although it's expensive, it's worth it, because our people are made to feel important...We might settle for one elegant banquet a year rather than two moderate ones."

One of the greatest needs we have is to receive recognition. So give people recognition! Draw attention to them so that others notice them! The fun part about recognition is that you have an infinite supply to draw from. It's like a smile: you can't run out, and it seems that people don't tire of them.

Of course, if you never give people corrective feedback, the value they put on your positive comments

> *People who feel good about themselves produce good results.*
> —Kenneth Blanchard, Author

diminishes. Don Clifton and Tom Rath, in their book, <u>How Full Is Your Bucket?</u>, suggest a magic 5:1 minimum ratio of positive to negative comments to build high trust relationships. (However, anything over a 13:1 ratio is perceived as insincere.)

Gallup Research has found that employees who receive regular recognition and praise:

- Increase their productivity
- Receive higher loyalty and satisfaction scores from customers
- Improve employee engagement among their colleagues
- Are more likely to stay with their organization

Here is a useful formula to recognize individual achievements:

WHAT YOU ACHIEVED	Betty, congratulations on achieving your sales goal this month.
THE VALUE YOU PROVIDED TO OTHERS	You have helped 48 new customers enjoy the benefits of owning and enjoying high-end bikes. The revenue is helping us profitably grow this business. Your leadership by example inspires all of us to higher achievement.
WHAT I ESPECIALLY APPRECIATE	I especially appreciate the way you work with our team. You are kind, thoughtful, and tons of fun. Betty, I am proud of you!

The power of positive affirming statements is foundational to building and sustaining healthy relationships. In 1992, John Gottman studied 700 couples who had just received their marriage licenses. Researchers video-taped a 15-minute conversation with each couple and counted the number of positive and negative interactions. Ten years later, based on the 5:1 magic ratio, researchers were 94% accurate in predicting which marriages would make it.

Celebrate the people in your business (and your life) by affirming them and their contributions.

> *"There are two things people want more than sex and money... recognition and praise."*
> —Mary Kay Ash, Founder
> Mary Kay Cosmetics

22

ACCELERATOR #3:

Learn from Your Experience

"The ability to learn faster than your competition may be the only sustainable competitive advantage."
—Arie DeGeus, Business Strategist

KENTUCKY IS THE HORSE CAPITAL of the world. When horse owners and breeders look for legal representation, they often call on Sturgill, Turner, Barker, and Maloney in Lexington, Kentucky. This progressive law firm has experienced the power of being on the same page.

Phil Maloney, the Managing Partner, says it's all about "working together with common goals and common values. We've been able to remove people's doubts. They trust themselves, each other, and management."

Phil goes on to say, "We focus on continuous improvement. We keep learning and growing. We take the time to encourage and recognize people's personal and professional achievements. We support each other out of our love for one another. It's good for our people, and it's good for our business."

For the past three years, they have been recognized as the #8, the #4, and the #1 Place to Work in Kentucky for companies under 250 employees.

> *In the best people I see a commitment to a continual learning.*
> —Paul O'Neill, Chairman and CEO Alcoa

PriorityRenewals™ are a great time to recognize people and encourage learning.

The question is how can you learn faster than your competitors? You can learn faster by learning from each other.

Now, to really get the value out of this, you must encourage people to *tell their stories.* Just sharing a general aphorism like "communication

> *The growth and development of people is the highest calling of leadership.*
> —Harvey Firestone, Founder Firestone Tire and Rubber Company

is important" isn't very helpful. However, learning that a key customer likes to be taken out to lunch once a year can be vital.

Here's a framework for sharing a lesson learned, briefly:

- Name the story.
- Share the context or situation.
- Describe what you or someone else did.
- Explain what happened as a result (could be good or bad).
- Summarize with the lesson learned.

Story Element	Example
Name the Story	Delegation Builds Trust
Situation or Context	"I often find myself doing work that I know could be done more efficiently and cost effectively by someone else.
What You Did	Recently, I decided to delegate a large amount of work to one of my colleagues.
Result	As I trusted them, they also trusted me. I had made a good decision! I was able to focus on higher leverage work, bring more value to our clients and our company.
Lesson Learned	Effective delegation to people of character and competence takes trust and builds trust."

It's also helpful to document these lessons. Write them down. Make them available to people. Good stories will be told and retold. Think of our sacred literature or our fairy tales. They teach us, and they continue to teach us as we explore their deeper meanings.

When you share stories and lessons learned, you accomplish several things. First, you accelerate the learning of the entire company. Not only do you learn from your own experiences but you learn from the experiences of everyone else. Everyone also learns how to tell stories, how to communicate, how to teach, and how to inspire others. You develop leaders.

> "Are you green and growing or ripe and rotting?"
> —Ray Kroc, Founder McDonalds

It's important not to rush this process. Learning, like a growing plant, follows a natural course. You can only provide the optimum environment for the plant to grow naturally—light, water, nutrients. Don't push too hard. People need to grow into sharing their learning.

As people start telling stories, they need to be encouraged. Clap a lot, and tell them, "Good story!" Make it a big deal, and you'll get more storytelling.

> *I do not think one can explain growth. It is silent and subtle. One does not keep digging up a plant to see how it grows.*
> —Emily Carr, Artist and Author

Create the environment for learning to take place. Keep recalling the lessons and you will find that you have a company that is not only learning, but is getting better at learning.

23

ACCELERATOR #4:

Evaluate Your Plan

"If the rate of change inside an organization is slower than the rate of external change—the end is near."
—Jack Welch, Chairman and CEO
General Electric

THE WORD "ENTREPRENEUR" WAS COINED by a French economist, Jean-Baptiste Say, in 1804. He said, "The entrepreneur shifts economic resources out of an area of lower productivity into an area of higher productivity and yield." The PriorityRenewal™ is an opportunity to shift resources and communicate changes that will better serve your customers and employees, and therefore, business owners.

When Jack Welch wanted to turn around the company founded by Thomas Edison in 1878, he said, "I want a revolution at GE. Let's go for it."

"In a time of drastic change, it is the learners who inherit the future. The learned usually find themselves equipped to live in a world that no longer exists."
—Eric Hofer, Businessman

He went on to say, "My job is to put the best people on the biggest opportunities and the best allocation of dollars in the right places. That's about it. Transfer ideas and allocate resources and get out of the way." Sometimes Jack Welch's type of revolutionary change is appropriate. Evolutionary change is always necessary.

Sesame Street has won more Emmys than any show in the history of television. In 1968, Joan Ganz Cooney, founded Sesame Street with

> *We are constantly challenging what we do—building a culture of restless self-renewal.*
> —Lou Gerstner, Chairman and CEO IBM

two goals: to entertain and educate children. "I was driven, almost from the time I graduated (college) by a sense of idealism and wanting to make some difference with my life," she said.

"Joan's been somebody who pushes for improvement," said Gary Knell, CEO of Sesame Workshop. "Other people would have retired, but she has a keen interest in not just keeping Sesame Street alive, but in keeping it vibrant. Joan has really, in many ways, kept us true to the brand and the trust that we've built with parents for now almost three generations."

As a group, look at your plan. Does it still work in today's environment? Does it need to change or be updated? Do the strategies still make sense? Are there new forces at work in your industry or market that you need to respond to? What is in your plan that needs to change? Adapting your plan to the changing marketplace ensures the long-term success of your organization.

This evaluation will demonstrate your ability—as a leader and as a team—to look at the "harsh reality" of your situation. Will you give it an honest and thorough appraisal or will you gloss over the rough spots in an attempt to avoid hurting people's feelings?

This can be a difficult step. The emergence from blissful ignorance to conscious pain is difficult on the ego. You may fear that you'll never emerge into competence. In reality, the opposite is the case. You can't emerge into competence until you admit how bad things are. As long as you're telling yourself that everything's O.K., you will never make the changes necessary to become competent.

You and your team need to face the harsh reality. Protecting yourself from the truth won't help you survive.

> *When you're through changing, you're through.*
> —Bruce Barton
> Advertising Executive

Over a period of several years, Ana Ochoa & Company reinvented itself. Ana's real estate business in Laredo, Texas, created an affiliation with Coldwell Banker, moved to new upscale offices, and replaced many of their agents. The business is performing better than ever and has significantly increased in value. PriorityRenewal™ is all about innovation—finding new and better ways to meet the needs of customers, employees, and owners.

24

ACCELERATOR #5:

Commit to New Priorities

*"If you go to work on your goals, your goals will go to work on you.
If you go to work on your plan, your
plan will go to work on you. Whatever good things we
build end up building us."*
—Jim Rohn, Business Philosopher

IN THE FALL OF 2003, MINAZ ABJI ACCEPTED the biggest challenge (and the biggest promotion) of his life. He moved from Vancouver, Canada to Washington, D.C. to become Executive Vice President of Asset Management for Host Hotels & Resorts. Through the interview process he knew he was going to be leading a highly competent, committed, and motivated group of individuals. What he didn't know was that the team was dysfunctional.

Dysfunctional? Yes. Minaz said, "They weren't living up to their potential. I discovered that this department never had a

> *"Plans are only good intentions unless they immediately degenerate into hard work."*
> —Peter Drucker
> Father of Modern Management

shared plan. So, I quickly organized a session to get my new team on the same page. We developed a Dynamic Business Growth Plan, including our vision, mission, and values. We discussed our issues and problems. We defined our objectives and strategies. We set priorities and got to work. We put the right people in the right positions."

Minaz was implementing PriorityAdvantage™. "The key," he said, "has been our Quarterly Renewals, where we

> *Since not all tasks are created equal, the organized executive must set priorities…*
> —Stephanie Winston, Author

regularly celebrate our progress, talk about what's working, what's not working, and what needs to be improved. We also set new priorities for the next quarter."

So what results were achieved at Host Hotels & Resorts?

- Improved financial performance. In four years, Host's share price rose two and a half times.

- Increased confidence. The team has developed a quiet self-assurance. They are consistently rated high on teamwork and job satisfaction by their clients and business partners.

- Capacity to grow. In 2006, Host acquired a group of hotels that increased their portfolio by 35% overnight. The integration wasn't without challenges, but it went smoothly.

- Effective partnering. Surveys with partners have shown significant gains in improved performance, satisfaction, and loyalty.

During a PriorityRenewal™, you may find that some of your old priorities need to carry forward. You may also find new ones that will now take precedence. In either case, you want a clear set of priorities for every person for the new achievement cycle.

> *Don't fear failure so much that you refuse to try new things. The saddest summary of a life contains three descriptions: could have, might have, and should have.*
> —Louis E. Boone
> Author and Educator

With a new set of priorities, you're off and running again.

EPILOGUE
Putting PriorityAdvantage™
to Work

"Well done is better than well said."
—Anonymous

IN OUR WORK WITH HUNDREDS OF COMPANIES over the years, we've noticed this progression:

Phase I - Organizations Solve Problems	Organizations go to work on solving their pressing problems and the issues that require immediate attention. As the leadership team masters this new set of skills and tools, PriorityAdvantage™ may seem somewhat mechanical.
Phase II – Organizations Build Capacity	Organizations expand their capacity, thereby enabling them to bring greater value to the marketplace. At this time, PriorityAdvantage™ is integrated into daily operations.
Phase III – Organizations Seize New Opportunities	Organizations seize new opportunities. Over time, PriorityAdvantage™ becomes the way of getting things done.

Over time, PriorityAdvantage™ becomes your business operating system and the system accelerates your growth. Here is an example of how this has worked for one company.

WGK Engineers, a highly respected civil engineering company in central Mississippi, wanted to make

> *Growing means the ability to deal with bigger, more complex problems.*
> —Ichak Adizes, Author

significant improvements in their business. In 2004, they engaged in the PriorityAdvantage™ process. They were at Phase I, Solving Problems. The owners focused on getting the right people in the right positions, unifying their team with their Dynamic Business Growth Plan, and increasing accountability. They also broke down the walls between their three business units. The three units became one functioning team.

And what happened? As individuals contributed in their area of strength and were accountable for their results, they became more productive. They got more work done. They began cleaning up messes and solving problems. As they addressed problems, they created more time to solve additional problems. By the end of Phase I, they were not facing as many crises as they used to. They actually found themselves with some extra time, and they started to think differently.

They entered Phase II of planning, which often tends to shift focus to improving processes. WGK's process improvement focused on:

- Billing
- Project Management
- Budgeting
- Surveying
- Management

As WGK improved their processes, they created more value for their customers and they reduced wasted time, effort, and money. As they did this, profits naturally improved. In fact, their profits increased by 400%

over the previous year. As they improved their processes, they prevented problems from occurring. They freed up even more time to solve bigger problems and seize new opportunities. They began to think about their business in ways they had never thought before.

In Phase III, WGK completed the largest design/build project in company history. "We had the capacity and the finances to handle it," said Greg Gearhart, Managing Partner. "We had our best year ever."

> *You can tell the "size" of a person by the "size" of the problems that preoccupy him.*
> —Ichak Adizes, Author

What happened was simple. The planning process developed into a virtuous cycle. One improvement led to another improvement which led to another improvement, and so on. Now, WGK has a system for constant improvement, learning, and growth.

WGK, like hundreds of other organizations, has engaged their employees and accelerated their growth. In doing so, they are continuously improving the quality of life and economic well-being for their customers, employees, and the owners. They are also developing leaders throughout the organization. Isn't that what business is all about?

NOW GO FOR IT!

YOU NOW HAVE AN EFFECTIVE AND DYNAMIC way to organize all the work in your company. This system will accommodate change and keep people on the same page.

When you practice PriorityPrinciples™, you learn and apply the fundamental principles that govern business success. You give generously, synergize your visionary and operational leaders, apply the 80/20 principle, involve your people, keep it clear and simple, follow a system, and go for progress, not perfection.

When you implement the second practice, PriorityPlanning™, you and your leadership team put all your desires and issues on the table. Then you sort through them, make some choices, and organize them into the six elements of a plan: vision, mission, values, objectives, strategies, and priorities.

Then you move to the practice of PriorityAchievement™. You focus on progress. You identify your most important priorities and appropriate action steps within a pre-determined time frame. You honor everyone's unique contributions, help them make progress, and improve relationships along the way.

By engaging in the practice of PriorityRenewal™, you step back and look at what you've accomplished and what you've learned. You celebrate the progress and share your lessons. You adapt your plan and set new priorities for the next achievement cycle.

This system provides the framework for getting people on the same page, setting and achieving priorities, celebrating progress, and adapting to the ever-changing marketplace. Leaders have a proven methodology to manage the entire enterprise. It's simple to understand and easy to teach, so you can quickly get everyone working with the same framework. That gives you time to focus your energy on building your business instead of trying to invent a system for running your business.

You now have a leadership system that's simple to create and easy to maintain. Now go for it!

ABOUT
JOE CALHOON

JOE CALHOON HAS SPENT THE PAST 25 years working with business owners and business leaders to develop higher performing organizations. His clients include some of the world's finest organizations, such as 3M, GE, Best Buy, Northwestern Mutual Life, and Ritz Carlton Hotels, as well as hundreds of small and medium-sized companies.

Joe's extensive business achievements enhance his professional communication skills. In addition to helping start more than 20 new business ventures in the solar and energy conservation industry, Joe was recognized as National Management Coordinator of the Year, and an Outstanding Young Man in America.

During the 1990's, Joe was the most requested and highest rated keynote speaker with Stephen Covey and the Covey Leadership Center. He has taught principles and practices of leadership and organizational performance on four continents.

Joe is a Certified Speaking Professional (CSP) with the National Speakers Association – an honor fewer than 500 of their 4,000 worldwide members have earned. In the past 25 years, he has given more than 2,500 presentations to 500 different organizations.

Joe is the co-founder of PriorityAdvantage™ and the co-author of Prioritize!–A System for Leading Your Business and Life on Purpose.

He lives with his wife, Diane, in Kansas City, Missouri.

ABOUT
BRUCE JEFFREY

BRUCE JEFFREY IS A BUSINESS COACH focused on developing personal success and high performance leadership teams.

For the past 20 years, Bruce has served to increase organizational performance through training, managing, leading, and consulting with a variety of organizations including Fortune 500's, medium-size companies, business start-ups, government, and non-profit organizations.

Some of Bruce's clients have included Sprint, Citicorp, Motorola, Ford Motor Company, Kimberly-Clark, Bank of America, DST Systems, Informix, Intercontinental Hotels, and Host Marriott.

Bruce has a unique ability to "clarify and simplify." He has guided a wide range of executive teams through the process of creating dynamic business growth plans, and then systematically executing that plan.

Bruce graduated summa cum laude from the Air Force Academy. He was recognized as "Outstanding Junior Officer of the Year" from his Flight Squadron. Bruce went on to lead the Training and Development effort for a company that grew by 300% in four years.

Bruce is the co-author of Prioritize!–A System for Leading Your Business and Life on Purpose.

Bruce and his wife, Bobbie, live in Kansas City, Missouri.

AFTERWORD

WE WOULD LOVE TO HEAR FROM YOU. As we work with companies, we learn from their experiences, and that helps us to refine our system. You have the benefit of learning from others, and they get the benefit of learning from you. So please contact us; we'd love to hear your story.

We also have many resources available to help you in your journey; some are free and some carry a modest investment. Of course, we also offer speaking, training, and consulting services to help you along your way. Please let us know how we can help you.

For more information, please visit our website at www.priorityadvantage.com or call 816-285-8144.

Our best to you!

—Joe and Bruce

NOTES